WITHERING SHELL

POORVA ARORA

Made with ❤ on the Notion Press Platform
www.notionpress.com

TO MY INSPIRATION WHO DIDN'T EVEN KNOW ME .

Contents

Contents

Foreword

Preface

<u>Books are sky, readers are the birds & writer is the creator of sky.</u>

Most probably you will ignore the front matter but if in case you read it

Then this is for you!

If everything goes simple forever then that is not less than a bald man crying daily for his hairs, but if he starts acting like he's having dark, shiny hairs and combing it everyday then this will make his life buzz. That is all needed!

Simple !

Imagine which you can't even imagine

This too apply for me I too imagine that I will write a book one day and that's what life is jerky!

If anything is not unpredictable then loose it instead of hanging it all the time.Somethings are meant for loosing not for hanging!

I spot light SOMETHINGS !

1. HAIRS

These little wires all juxtaposed
Inhancing the living

Matching the vibes
So childlike!

Spreaded all over cohesively
Beating with the birds

All imersely dipped in the talk with gale
When tied up make an aversion

Hit so hard that falls on the ground
So childlike!

Have different - different colours
But shows same friendship

Always are messed
But sounds so blessed

In love with everything they're in touch

When personified they are not less than a lover

So childlike ♥

2. ACCEPT-ED

The loathe
The beauty
The sitch
Everything everyone is exceptional
You don't know me
I don't know you
Whilst we don't know self
You'll involve in me
I'll deep dive in you
You'll get sick
I'll get tired
It'll end
Except expectations
Time will spill on expectations
besides
It'll forget things
Forgetting reduces agony
Agony will left stain of expectations
&
It'll needed to accept-ed
In lieu of except-it

3. DISPERSION

Messed up amongst all
Heavy like jumbo jet
Where's the way
No idea!!

Mismanaging everything
I could bear
And dissolving whole day
In tears

Cravings are greatest foe
And mind is greatest sin

Illusionsing for oneself
That it's kintsugi...

But inner self screams
What you have left out
Is all dispersion

Which will dismissed
When light (life) gets off...

4. BLUE

Blue
A sign of aversion

But hold sanctity
And behold indulgence

First exposure to nature
Is routed through sky

The 1st sight impel to sky- high
The 1st warmth touch aspire to be mushy

Blue water
Incline to enrich ally

To glide on love &
To swirl on loathe

To feel densely every emotion
To be pure

To scrabble every little joy

To be brawny in every big war

To mother wit every stupidity
&
To endure every abhor
Blue is poetic!

5. LIFE AS A WRITER

Life as a writer

So passionate
life is about writing

Writing such a big scriptures
With so much patience

Handling coming obstacles
Surmising exotic adventures
depicting belle

With a clench fist
Ribbon on head
& a wand scribbling magic

Clearing
All dull superstition about a writer

Showing his great work
With great confidence

Mannualy describing all fancy themes
Which we can admire with sort of time

Adding ample value in sample time
Aspiring a long & exciting struggle
&
Inspiring for miracle

He's really a cliff hanger ?

6. BUTTERFLY

Not entitled with any title

Not in rage
Or with love
I can be arrested

Neither sky
or land
Nothing belongs to me
Nor I do

Me as an deaf
Just movin forward ➡
like a dumb
Reacting to pessimist

With Amber eyes

Just
Squizing all
Seizing all

Me as a butterfly
Moving ahead & ahead

To just
Squizing all
Seizing all

7. GALE

Bygone in the creation
Nipper in the walk

Always calms inner thunder
But responsible for outer twister

Is invisible but palpable
Involved with in without a clape

But gives thunder when
Becomes a thunderclap

Make you feel better
when sucked
Make you realize
The importance of butterfly effect

Pushes the melancholy away
Hedging the hub of bad ideas

Involves you with you
&

Make you realize about
The beautiful eyes
THAT TELL LIES

8. PATTERNS

Patterns are alluring

Lungs carry same pattern
As a tree do
And both are essential for each other

We are connected to everything
Everything is connected to us

Solitude spots the pattern
Togetherness enhance the pattern

We are drived by the heart
Heart is companion of brain
Brain is champ of us!

We do hate
We do love
We die to do
We do to die

Starting is lively

End is lonely

Pattern is same
Serene needs zest
Zest needs serene!!

9. PERCEPTION

Halloween is daunting
Or beginning of new eve
It depends on
Perception

Alike sages
We too have
Obsession
(social media)
Too depend on perception

In every step forward
We have proportion of
Everything

Than too we go up in smoke
For which
We get less in proportion
Too depend on perception

Everything is perception of
Not having a perception

And to ignite
When said
You have different perception

10. FLOW

Flow is a natural being
Either it's a wish
or
Consequence

It can't be done in flow
When you mean it
&
Often it's a boon
to creator

Somethings meant to be
Done in flow
But
Not everytime
This magic works

It's enigma
Out of wits

Once broken
Can't scribble

That magic again

Because it's not a wish
But a consequence

11. WHY NOT FOR LIFE

Clear sky talks more
Clearer of all facts
Wanted to know more
Clear things moves up
Above the water
Above the sky
Above the mind
Heavier things
Bow you down
Either it's a relation or respect
Junk is always filtered
Either it's a water or files
Than
Why not for life

12. DOVE

New you new me
Everything chic
We'll make

Unlike old one
Everything bright
We'll make

Boy to man
Girl to woman

We'll act as
Steward for green self

Dove
Alike us
We'll make

Love ♥
Alike dove
We'll make

Wonder how blossom

Our adventure

We'll make

13. WEIRDO

Little things of
Weirdo
I'm half way done
& amidst
I'm leaving it
Just for boredom

Don't know why
Hitting swings
In every 3 seconds

Now that much weird
That counting
On fingers

Covering a long way
With short temper
Discreet of Simpness
Fond of sternness

I'm not spoiled
But rotten amongst

My fellow stars ?

I didn't have affinity
In me!
In me
I carry solitude

Stirring my insecurities
So mould into
Boldness

Just little things
Of weirdo

14. BLACK HOLE

Eyes are galaxy
With the black hole
In middle

All reasons of attraction
Is black hole

Once dipped
Can't return

Once sink
Can't tell what happened

Time stops
We stay same
As we were

Neither we deteroit
Nor upgrade

But when we return
All get changed

You were
Not destroyed
But
Other kicked upstairs

That's the reason for devastation
THE BLACK HOLE

15. UNITY IS IMPORTANT

Unity is important
When you draws
your head on life ..

When you withdraw
every of your moves
from your box

Not just
You need to win
But
To become indespensible

Not from outer layer (body)
But from inner soil(soul)

Become like
No one was there like you
before you

Unity is important
Not from else
But
From your inner wealth

UNITY IS IMPORTANT

16. BARE FOOTED

Clumsily
Beating with the rain
With an aesthetic smile
&
Rosy cheeks ☺

Riding
Bare footed
&
exploring
Different shades
of feelings

Sensing ..
The rain drops
Discerning ..
The wet sand

With a soft touch of zephyr

All
Nudging to

POORVA ARORA

Grin like a Cheshire cat ?

17. WITHERING SHELL

Doesn't matter
How hard a shell seams
At a time
It also kneel down

Doesn't matter
How gloomy withering heard
After a time
It gives some other a new life

It's an itsy bitsy chaos
That is beyond one to understand

By resisting the slopes
It makes one well built

By enduring the virtue
It makes one dim

So ironical everything seems

It's a part of hustle
&
Ensue of bustle ❤

18. MOON

Writing
Letter to the Moon

Firstly I wonder
to define your beauty

But that's nasty
It's feisty to
just be a gossiper with you

How these all changed
You witnessed it all

Heaven into hell
&
Hell into heaven
All creeping

Just writing this crap
To answer my solitude

Completing

my years old remaining work
Beneath the shadow of shyness
I leaved it undefined

But shyness is turning into slyness

Like me you are too
engulfed with loads of stars
But I respect your solitude

Your every phase
from full moon to crescent
and to eclipse
murmur every of your swings

That shows you are not less than a human

You spread light of sun
Peeps laugh on you
Because they are unaware of

You can see your brighter side more easily in the shadow of moon
rather than of sun

THAT'S THE POWER OF PEACE ♥

19. PERFECTLY IMPERFECT

I don't know what I am

Good or bad
Bad or worse

Or deep down that

Sometimes meek
(I don't want)

Sometimes stiff
(I don't want)

Somewhere social
Somewhere antisocial
&
Somewhere restrained

What the hell I'm
Wanna know but don't know what

& that what makes me hell
Throne of extreme feelings

Dipping deep down in

Impulsive for bursting
But lacking impulsiveness ..

20. CLOWN

Blunder of thoughts
Swirling around

So airy
These thoughts are

When get attention
Jump onto the next

If not,
Keep bumping you
Till not get

Can't conclude
what they are about

They are clown
Acrobating in my brain

Can't say who will be their ringleader
But for sure I'm only the audience

They have
A serious platonic relationship with me

Never leaves me aloof
&
I can't even condemn

As it is platonic not erotic.

21. THE WRITER

The one
who can reveal anything
Murmuring in her head!

.

Make feel detached when terraced
And
Terraced when detached

.

refine the emotions like blossom
Can influence minds and heart ♥
All without any ideas

.

Embrace sitch with words
And soul with emotions

.

Is the one who evince
Aesthetic in everything!!...

22. ARCHITECTURE

Nothing in this world
Can be faded...
Everything is so peaceful

.

Architecture of this house
Must get an Oscar..
Even more than that!!

.

The breezes, the mountains, insects small like ant big like us,
The emotions in these puff (anger, happiness, exuberance, humanity...)
Everything is so peaceful..

.

But
Anything can never be perfect.
Even the moon have moles..
In this so called 'perfectionist world'
We have one taint..

.

Just like fake powers in every south movies
Every insect in this universe
Also have fake ego..

Someone have bigger
Some carry smaller
We can do compare it
Because
We also have competitiveness as an emotion

But then too...
Architecture of this house must get an Oscar
But NOT more than that!!

23. NATAL DAY

We A SOUL!!
Unknown of reason of our existence
Celebrating fantasy..

.

Fantasy of ACHIEVEMENT
Delusion of LOVE
Fallacy of BIRTH

.

Blissing out on the mishappening
Hedging all the gospels (God's truth)

.

Living this shit
and
Walking on air
For
Living this shit

.

Making again a old wives tale ♥
On every birthday Eve
&
Just Doing these lunatic things
Just to hear HAPPY BIRTHDAY ?

24. YOU!

Years & years rolled on..
We met and separate ?

No room for any feelings
We said...
But coincidentally, we aggregate

Words go and hide
You are too less to admire

Sparks on our faces
is enough to aspire ..

Daily knocking down serene of mind
Embracing sentiments enough to refine

Making such a dumb hallucination
But
Hoping it to be turned in reality for forever

Manning janitor
To keep you away

But thoughts report no janitor ?

25. EMOTIONS

Twinkle of ignite emotions
Asking for hiding
But
Lacking childhood

Asking for enduring
But
Lacking fadness

Asking for manning little gold
But
Lacking inactivity..

Now getting plumpy
Asking to rupture
No one cares

Asking to erupt
No one cares

Then ejected the nouse
Spread melancholy

But

No one cares!!

26. PAL

Tap of feather seems
You are admiring me

Sprint of rain feels
You are fusing with me

Dazzling voice of air
Utters every gossip you had for me &?

Every beat of lightning feels that
You are dancing with me ?

In every emotion
In every state ?

I had seen you as pal
&
Had sense you palpably.....

27. MYSTERIES

Mysteries are hidden
As it's their nature
They are superficially deep rooted ?

They are mysteries brother
They weave a giant maze

They are on-going boon
But seen as renunciator

Mysteries give bolt from blue
When hitted,
Whom hitted
No idea!

They facinate love from lives
& unleash eyeball from eye ?

It's too arrogant to argue about superstitions
But some superstitions are damn bold
That gives a high volt ??

28. INSANE

Cringy grin
Is all I need
Then comes a label
INSANE
That I hate outmost
Covering all my heart ♥
I called it obedient
But
That doesn't merry
With sprint of jolliness
I hovered around reluctance
Gradually
Getting annoyed
Now that much
That everything seems insane
And than too
I'm reluctant
Of being insane....

29. THE SOUND

Where every thing is quite
Than there's a noise

Breath
Rain
Zephyr

Everything express
Their jolliness

Inviting us to be a part of them
To keep still for seconds
And be relaxed for centuries

Discern every glimpse
&
Adore every friendliness
Of every freak

Everyone have their stories

And the best part is

Everything is same

Except the sound (emotional imbalance)

30. ALONE

Alone
With all darkness
Shades of darkness
can be spotted now

This ditch is Soo deep
Where I can't found myself
Twice
With all the irony
I'm introducing with
Now,
I think low spirit is friend of mine

How's that everything going ahead
But I'm there at the back
Spoiling there
Alone!

How can someone be so miserable
Unaware of what's happening
Still holding foes
That sucks

That's woeful
All alone!!

31. BEING DIFFERENT

In the race of being different
When will I win
Lunate amongst all
When will i win

So insane this all seams
When mood twists
From level up joy to down misery

What incarnate I embody
Where's the secret
even I don't know

But I'm stuck on his ego
Where's the way
Of being different
Of being butterfly
So that I can too fly high
Make the sky short
&
My wing long

How to do friendship
With this bitter soul
Seeming like a hell
But yet have to spend whole life with

Who can't even see
How much burden it's giving

Instead of "being"
I'm busy in "seeing"
THE DIFFERENCE
OF BEING DIFFERENT!!

32. A MAN

A freaking jerk
Now an adult
With an ruthless eyes ?

Now it's savouring
Like hell
Appeals not to rebel
It will cause mess
Blank head
With
Burdened heart

No support
No kindness
Just entitled
As spoiled brat

When an hope alters
Named as flirt
When tried to rebate ourself
Labelled as tactless

Asked to be fearless
Can't embody soft side
It'll named as cowardice

Jump into furnace
For everyone's safety
After compromising
Every of merry

This will be called man
Who forgo everything
But can't display
As its his duty
Because he's A MAN ?

33. IMAGINATION

In which we live is all imagination
There's
No locations
No superstitions
No money

We have made these patterns
Everything is in mind

Rules
Limitations
Faith
Loyalty
Royalty

Everything is imaginary
Can't be seen in monkey's group

We all work for a pattern
To make something suitable
To someone

Someone is working in a pattern
For making something suitable
For someone

More we contribute
More we regain

More we imagine
More we thrive

34. BLURRY

Sometimes blur images too give a dense vibe
sometimes being blurry is good

Ignoring the goofy shits
It penetrate romance of a freak

Disagreeing all true bedlam
Focusing to find aesthetic in everything

True notion can be heart broken
but being blurry is sunset in drizzle!

35. DANCE LIKE A PEACOCK

Dance like a peacock

Sway with breezes
Stay with weather

Let
Sprinkle sence you
Spirit go pink
&
Time go foil

Re-gain all cherished moments
Re-live wizard chore
&
Re-value love

With a swift desire to shine
Go with your pace

Zest like a fat cat ?

POORVA ARORA

&

GLEAM LIKE A STAR ?

36. AUGUST

No destination to reach upon ..

Standin still as upronting
THE ELEPHANT'S FOOT
And
Going ahead as
XENON GAS

No idea of
Whether it'll Take me to clouds
Or
Will bury me deep inside
Well..
I'm not samosely
But
To me it seems flamboyant

Exploding in me as it did in Chernobyl (1986)

Without knowing its dispatching me & I'm savouring it..

It's preparing to cremate me

But it's pleasing to me
As late to this date it's going to
AUGUST ME

37. DESTINY

What a romance of destiny is...

When you get attached
It shows you
how small droplets
Also have to leave their cloud

When you get detached
It shows how badly
these tiny bumps falls

It teaches you not to trust
(Ravan carry off Sita)
On contrary!
It asks you to have faith
(our brave scriptures)

Destiny in simpler terms is reflection of past..
And
One for no reason!

There's nothing as destined legacy

I'm what I'm today because of the choices I made yesterday!!!

38. DOWDY

Knowingly doing bitter things...
Asking for a miracle, or
For God's favour
Is so dowdy!!!
Having a shit like this is disgraceful
Making ecstatic moves is not enough for me
I think...
There's something missing..
I feel
Beneath all unpleasant experiences
There's something gracious..
But my brain is too ignite
That's also my fault!!
Agreeing on everyone's perception is not my lady....
But
That thirst of bursting emotions is.....

39. ME,MINE,MYSELF

Me, mine,myself
These words bow me down
Or make my head in clouds

Mirroring myself isn't easy
It takes one whole life
To be myself

Everyday new sins
I discover
Everyday new wings
I discover

Everyday
I leave a note for my younger self
To appreciate or to negotiate

I wait everyday
To read myself

Ignoring is easy
But

Dealing with myself
Is chaotic

Coz it takes
One whole life
To make me myself!

40. SUPERFLUOUS EXAGGERATIONS

Superfluous Exaggerations
Hit em hard
Alot to say
Then keep quiet
In a fear
It will start a
Superfluous Conversation
Above my head
There's my over exaggerations
From where starts my hesitation
Prerequisites Everywhere,
Boxing someone's ear
For making
Own
superfluous exaggerations
But
Was I wrong
To be shrewd
When thinking off
Of my favorite situation

The superfluous exaggerations

9 798888 837122

Printed by Libri Plureos GmbH in Hamburg,
Germany